D1366463

KOBE BRYANT

A Real-Life Reader Biography

John Torres

Mitchell Lane Publishers, Inc.
P.O. Box 619 • Bear, Delaware 19701

www.mitchelllane.com

Printing   3   4   5   6   7   8   9   10

Real-Life Reader Biographies

Paula Abdul	Christina Aguilera	Marc Anthony	Lance Armstrong
Drew Barrymore	Tony Blair	Brandy	Garth Brooks
Kobe Bryant	Sandra Bullock	Mariah Carey	Aaron Carter
Cesar Chavez	Roberto Clemente	Christopher Paul Curtis	Roald Dahl
Oscar De La Hoya	Trent Dimas	Celine Dion	Sheila E.
Gloria Estefan	Mary Joe Fernandez	Michael J. Fox	Andres Galarraga
Sarah Michelle Gellar	Jeff Gordon	Virginia Hamilton	Mia Hamm
Melissa Joan Hart	Salma Hayek	Jennifer Love Hewitt	Faith Hill
Hollywood Hogan	Katie Holmes	Enrique Iglesias	Allen Iverson
Janet Jackson	Derek Jeter	Steve Jobs	Alicia Keys
Michelle Kwan	Bruce Lee	Jennifer Lopez	Cheech Marin
Ricky Martin	Mark McGwire	Alyssa Milano	Mandy Moore
Chuck Norris	Tommy Nuñez	Rosie O'Donnell	Mary-Kate and Ashley Olsen
Rafael Palmeiro	Gary Paulsen	Colin Powell	Freddie Prinze, Jr.
Condoleezza Rice	Julia Roberts	Robert Rodriguez	J.K. Rowling
Keri Russell	Winona Ryder	Cristina Saralegui	Charles Schulz
Arnold Schwarzenegger	Selena	Maurice Sendak	Dr. Seuss
Shakira	Alicia Silverstone	Jessica Simpson	Sinbad
Jimmy Smits	Sammy Sosa	Britney Spears	Julia Stiles
Ben Stiller	Sheryl Swoopes	Shania Twain	Liv Tyler
Robin Williams	Vanessa Williams	Venus Williams	Tiger Woods

Library of Congress Cataloging-in-Publication Data

Torres, John Albert

    Kobe Bryant / John Torres.

        p. cm. — (A real-life reader biography)

    Includes index.

    ISBN 1-58415-030-0

    1. Bryant, Kobe, 1978—Juvenile literature. 2. Basketball players—United States—Biography—Juvenile literature. [1.Bryant, Kobe, 1978- 2. Basketball players. 3. Afro-Americans—Biography.] I. Title. II. Series.

GV884.B794 T67 2000

796.323'092—dc21

[B]

                        36242060338809

                                              00-036534

ABOUT THE AUTHOR: John A. Torres is a newspaper reporter for the Poughkeepsie Journal in New York. He has written eleven sports biographies, including *Greg Maddux* (Lerner), *Hakeem Olajuwon* (Enslow), and *Darryl Strawberry* (Enslow). He lives in Fishkill, New York with his wife and two children. When not writing, John likes to spend his time fishing, coaching Little League baseball, and spending time with his family.

PHOTO CREDITS: Cover: Tom Hauck/Allsport; p.4 Corbis/Greg Allen; p. 6 John Gichigi/Allsport; p. 11 Fitzroy Barrett/ Globe Photos; p. 14 Reuters/Archive Photos; p. 18 Reuters/Mike Blake/Archive Photos; p. 23 Bruce Cotler/Globe Photos; p. 27 John Gichigi/Allsport; p. 28 Harry How/Allsport

ACKNOWLEDGMENTS: The following story has been thoroughly researched, and to the best of our knowledge, represents a true story. While every possible effort has been made to ensure accuracy, the publisher will not assume liability for damages caused by inaccuracies in the data, and makes no warranty on the accuracy of the information contained herein.

Table of Contents

Chapter 1
Basketball in His Blood

It was probably in January of 1997 that Kobe Bryant finally realized he had made the right decision. In fact, it was January 28, in Dallas, Texas, where the extremely young National Basketball Association rookie decided to make the All-Star Weekend his very own personal stage.

Even though the NBA junior had not actually been chosen to play in the All-Star Game itself, he had been chosen to participate in some of the weekend's activities. Not only did he participate, but he practically dominated the weekend.

Kobe made the January 1997 All-Star Weekend his very own personal stage.

Kobe in Milan for the Adidas Streetball Challenge.

On the Saturday before the regular All-Star Game, Kobe was the standout player of the Rookie Game with an event-record 31 points. Then, a few hours after the game, in an impressive show of airborne acrobatics, Kobe returned to the arena to become the first Los Angeles Laker ever to win the slam-dunk contest.

Kobe had easily won over the fans during the Rookie Game and then with his dominance of a contest that such great players as Michael Jordan and Dominique Wilkins had won before him. In that contest each player gets six chances to wow the judges with an array of spectacular dunks. Kobe saved the best for last when he posted 49 points out of a possible 50 in the final round of the dunking contest. One of the highlights was a whirling 360-degree jumping dunk that just electrified the crowd.

It was obvious that Kobe Bryant belonged in the NBA and clearly was among its youngest and brightest stars. Whoever had not yet heard of the high-school kid who had skipped college and gone right into the NBA heard of him now. Up until that point, Kobe would sometimes wonder if had made the right decision by not going to college and by entering the NBA draft at a very young age.

That sort of electrifying, dominating player was exactly what Lakers general manager and Hall-of-Famer Jerry West had envisioned just a few months earlier when he engineered a draft-day trade with the Charlotte Hornets for Kobe Bryant. It seemed as if everybody but West had been wondering whether the young player was ready for life in the NBA. After all, Kobe had never even set foot on a college basketball floor.

It was obvious that Kobe Bryant belonged in the NBA.

West wanted to pick Kobe early in the 1996 draft, but the Lakers did not have a high draft pick. West knew that a player like Kobe could be a cornerstone of a franchise that was trying to rebuild for the 1990s after winning several NBA championships in the 1980s. So he talked the Charlotte Hornets into taking journeyman center Vlade Divac for the youngster.

As Kobe Bryant continues to develop into one of the best players the NBA has seen in a long time—some people even call him the next Michael Jordan—Divac now plays for the Sacramento Kings. Some now say that the Bryant-Divac trade is possibly one of the worst basketball transactions of all time by the Charlotte team.

But, some would argue, anyone who knew anything about Kobe Bryant knew that he was bound to succeed. After all, he had basketball in his blood.

Chapter 2
A Big Move

Sometime in 1978, Kobe's parents, Joe and Pamela Bryant, were eating dinner at a restaurant. Pamela was pregnant. She had a craving for a steak dinner. The couple was looking at the menu while discussing what they would name their child if it were a boy.

Who would have guessed that they would find the name of their next child just by looking at a menu? They noticed a type of steak named Kobe. They ordered it, ate it, and decided to name their son after it. "It's true, he was named after a Kobe Steak House in King

"He was named after a Kobe Steak House in King of Prussia, Pennsylvania."

Shortly after learning how to walk, Kobe was learning how to shoot a basketball.

of Prussia, Pennsylvania," laughed his father.

Kobe was born in Philadelphia, Pennsylvania, on August 23, 1978. By that time, his father was an established NBA player.

Joe "Jellybean" Bryant was not an all-star, but he was a solid NBA player who was known as a defensive specialist. This meant that his team would often assign him to guard the opposing team's best-scoring player. He used those skills, as well as his athleticism and good basketball fundamentals, to play for many years. He played small forward and shooting guard for the Golden State Warriors, Philadelphia 76ers, and Houston Rockets. He wanted his son to follow in his footsteps.

When Kobe was only three years old, his dad set up a mini basketball hoop and put a basketball in the boy's hands. Shortly after learning to walk, Kobe was learning how to shoot a basketball.

When Kobe was born, he already had two older sisters, Sharia and Shaya. Because they were in a basketball family, they were used to moving around. Just a short time after Kobe was born, the family moved from Philadelphia to Houston so that they could all be close together. Little did they know they would soon be moving very far away.

Kobe and his two sisters are very close.

Kobe practically grew up on the basketball court, hanging out with his dad and dad's teammates. Sometimes he would even get to shoot on the court. By the time he was six years old, Kobe and his father were inseparable. The year was 1984, and Joe's NBA basketball career was coming to an end.

But Joe was not ready to quit basketball altogether. He knew that he could still make a lot of money playing—somewhere. He explored his options. There were semi-pro leagues and minor leagues in the United States, such as the Continental Basketball Association and the United States Basketball League. But Joe learned that he could make more money overseas.

In late 1984, Joe decided to move his family to Italy, where he could continue to play professional basketball. It turned out to be a great move for him and his family, and they would spend the next seven years there.

It wasn't easy at first for Kobe and his family. They had to adapt to a new country, a new culture, and, of course, a new language. But looking back now, Kobe loved those days.

"I loved growing up in Italy," he said. "I have always had a special place in my heart for the country and its people."

Chapter 3
Life in Italy

Kobe's father became a very popular player in Italy. The Italian people are passionate about soccer and basketball, and the towns follow their teams very closely. They cheer and chant as they wave flags and watch their favorite teams play. Joe was a fan favorite: the fans even incorporated his name into several team-spirit songs.

Adjusting to life in a different country, especially one where there are very few people of African descent actually helped draw the family closer together. For a while, before they learned how to speak Italian, they spoke

Adjusting to life in a different country helped draw the family closer together.

Kobe's childhood in Italy helped train him for the NBA.

only among themselves. It was a closeness born out of necessity.

"In that environment, where few people spoke English, we communicated a lot more," said Joe. "We had to."

Kobe's parents enrolled all three children in Italian-speaking parochial schools rather than in English-speaking schools. They wanted their kids to be able to fit in in their newly adopted country. This was a bit harder for Kobe's older sisters, but Kobe was still young enough to pick up the foreign language quickly.

"It wasn't hard," Kobe said. "When I was learning to read and write in first grade, so were all the other kids. It's just that we were doing it in Italian."

Kobe watched his father play a lot of basketball, and his dad taught him technical skills as well as the fundamentals of the game. He taught Kobe how to keep his arms up and how to shuffle his feet on defense. He taught him how to land after a jump shot and where to position himself for a rebound. He taught him how to box out and how to work on his leaping skills. Kobe would also spend time watching videos and reading articles about American basketball stars like Michael Jordan, Magic Johnson, and Larry Bird.

Kobe would study the videos and read the articles and imitate the things he learned. He spent a lot of time alone: after doing his homework and his daily chores, he would spend hour after hour dribbling the basketball on grassy soccer fields.

Sometimes kids would come over and ask Kobe to play soccer with them. Because he was already tall for his age and because he was quick on his feet and very athletic, Kobe made a perfect

Kobe would spend hour after hour dribbling the basketball on grassy soccer fields.

goalie. He would stand tall in the goal and deflect shot after shot. His new friends marveled at his quickness and agility.

Kobe looks back fondly at his time spent in Italy, but the memories are sometimes bittersweet. He had to grow up fast, aware of his differences, and learn how to spend time alone.

> **Kobe had to grow up fast, aware of his differences, and learn how to spend time alone.**

"Growing up in Italy, I became more of an individual," Kobe said. "The hardest thing in life is to know yourself and to master your emotions. And I learned those things from a very young age."

The Bryant family stayed close, and by the time Joe's playing days in Italy were over, they had become a very strong unit. Although the family was finally ready to settle down, Joe still had basketball in his system. He decided to try his hand at coaching.

It was back to the United States for them, and back to Philadelphia.

Chapter 4
Creating His Own Beat

Moving back to the United States and fitting in was not easy for Kobe. His sisters did okay, and his father took a job coaching basketball at La Salle University. But Kobe had a hard time.

The family moved to an affluent area of Pennsylvania called Lower Merion. Most of the kids there were white, and the few African-American kids had a hard time understanding why Kobe was so different. But he was. After all, he was a black 13-year-old who had been raised in a foreign country. He did not know much about rap music or even American pop. His

Kobe had a hard time moving back to the United States.

Kobe's hard work and dedication have made him successful.

English was not that great, and when he did speak English it was with a thick Italian accent.

But that was not the worst of it. Kobe was even starting to feel out of place in the one spot in the world where he was normally comfortable— the basketball court. In Europe, basketball, much like hockey, is more of a finesse game than it is here in the United States. This means the Europeans rely more on quickness and passing and even prefer to play in a slower version of the game.

The first few times he was on the court in Philadelphia, Kobe was out of sorts. But, much like he was forced to do in Italy, he learned to adapt to his new environment.

"At first I got my butt kicked in basketball because everything in Philly was more physical and up-tempo," Kobe said. "The beat was a little different. So I decided to create my own beat."

Create his own beat he did, with a little help from his dad.

Joe arranged for Kobe to practice with the La Salle basketball team and even sometimes with his old team, the Philadelphia 76ers. Not many 14- or 15-year-olds can boast about having scrimmaged with an NBA team. But Kobe could, and the lessons he learned have proved invaluable. He learned how to combine the finesse of European basketball, the street moves of the

The first few times he was on the court in Philadelphia, Kobe was out of sorts.

Philadelphia playgrounds, and the ruggedness and physical style of the NBA.

Kobe soon became a star at Lower Merion High School, where he broke every basketball record at the school. In fact, he was the all-time leading scorer in Southeastern Pennsylvania high school history with 2,883 points—breaking the mark of NBA legend Wilt Chamberlain, among others. He led his team to an incredible 77-13 record during his last three seasons and was a four-year starter on the varsity team.

As a high-school senior, Kobe received many accolades and honors as he simply dominated the competition. He was selected by *USA Today* and *Parade Magazine* as the National High School Player of the Year. He was also named Naismith Player of the Year, Gatorade Circle of Champions High School Player of the Year, and to the McDonald's All-American team.

As a senior he averaged 30.8 points per game and led his team to a state title

Kobe broke every basketball record at Lower Merion High School.

and a 31-3 record. He scored 50 points in a single game during the state playoffs.

Many colleges with great basketball programs, including Duke, Kentucky, Michigan, and La Salle, heavily recruited the youngster. Soon it would be time for him to make a very big decision.

Many colleges heavily recruited Kobe.

Chapter 5
A Tough Decision

Kobe knew that he could handle himself on the basketball court with NBA players.

In 1996, Kobe Bryant was faced with the biggest decision of his life: what college he would attend to earn a degree and maybe a ticket to the NBA. He had been watching the progress of another former high-school star who had decided to skip college and go right into the NBA: Kevin Garnett. The Minnesota Timberwolves star seemed to have made the transition from high-school to professional basketball with relative ease.

But Kobe knew that everybody was different. Yet he also knew that he was able to handle himself on the basketball court with NBA players. After all, he had scrimmaged with them for the past few years.

Once Kobe made up his mind, there

In 1996, Kobe took Brandy to his high school prom.

was no going back. He decided to skip college and apply for the NBA draft.

"This was my gut feeling," he later explained. "This is what I felt in my heart was the best thing for me to do, and there was no second-guessing."

Once Kobe declared himself eligible for the draft, Lakers general manager Jerry West, who had followed Kobe's career throughout high school, flew Kobe to Los Angeles for a workout. He could not believe his eyes as Kobe wowed him and other Lakers officials, including former NBA great Magic Johnson. However, West was not surprised at Kobe's great crossover dribble and court savvy. "See, the kids in America don't do the work that Kobe did," he said.

Kobe agreed. Those years in Italy had helped make him a better player. "When I was eight years old, they put me in a higher league with fourteen- and fifteen-year-olds," he said. "They were much bigger than I was."

West engineered the draft-day trade with the Hornets, and in July 1996 Kobe Bryant became a member of the Los Angeles Lakers.

Suddenly this young man, who still enjoyed watching his favorite movie, *Star Wars,* over and over again, was an NBA basketball player. Most kids his age were worried about dating or picking the right career path. Kobe was dunking basketballs with Shaquille O'Neal.

The Lakers wanted to bring Kobe along slowly, but he was too talented to keep on the bench. It is very rare that an NBA rookie is allowed to contribute to his team right away. But Kobe has always been different.

Playing at shooting guard, point guard, and small forward, Kobe appeared in 71 games during his rookie season and even started six of them. He averaged 7.6 points a game.

But he seemed to gain much more confidence after dominating that All-Star Weekend in Texas. He played much better during the second half of the season. In fact, on April 8 against the Golden State Warriors, he scored 24 points when he made nine of 11 shots.

He was voted to the NBA's All-Rookie Second Team, and the Lakers knew the best was yet to come.

The Lakers wanted to bring Kobe along slowly, but he was too talented to keep on the bench.

Chapter 6
Kobe's Vision

In the 1997–98 season the Lakers still wanted to bring Kobe off the bench. After all, he was still much younger than just about every other player in the league. There was plenty of time to cultivate his talents. Kobe became an expert sixth man. In basketball the first player off the bench is known as the sixth man. Usually this spot is reserved for a talented rookie or a player who can provide the team with some quick points. Kobe was both.

In 79 games, starting only one, Kobe improved his scoring average to 15.4 points per game while really

> **Kobe was still much younger than just about every other player in the league.**

working hard to improve just about every facet of his game. While Kobe's game continued to improve, something else remarkable happened. Kobe suddenly became one of the most popular figures in the game. Maybe it was because of his high-flying dunks. Maybe it was because of his infectious smile. Or maybe it was because he symbolized every kid's dream: a kid who still liked to play video games had

Kobe's skills always amaze his fans.

Kobe always tries to have fun on the court.

gone straight from high school to NBA stardom. But most of all, it was probably because NBA fans could see that Kobe Bryant really loved the game of basketball and was trying his best to always have fun.

"My father always played with a great love for the game and that's one of the things he always taught me," Kobe said. "He told me not to let the pressure or the expectations take away from my love for the game. I think that's the best advice anyone has ever given me."

The fans voted him to the All-Star team, where he became the youngest player ever to participate in the annual classic. He even scored a team-high 18 points in the game.

The next year NBA players went on strike; they played a shortened season once the labor dispute was over. It was Kobe's third NBA season and he had emerged as a team leader. The Lakers could no longer afford to use such a talented player as a sixth man. Kobe was made a starting guard, sometimes shifting between point guard and shooting guard. He started all 50 games and averaged just a shade below 20 points a contest.

Kobe was an expert at using his crossover dribble to drive to the basket and draw fouls. Teams were having a hard time stopping him. In one game, on April 11, Kobe scored 29 points and had five rebounds and five steals as the Lakers edged out the New York Knicks.

Kobe was an expert at using his cross-over dribble to drive to the basket and draw fouls.

Kobe helped lead the Lakers to a playoff appearance, but they were no match for the San Antonio Spurs, who went on to win the NBA Championship. But in 2000, expectations all over the league were very high for the Lakers. Many people expect them to make it to the NBA Finals.

Kobe's appeal continues to grow as he appears in many television commercials for soft drinks and sneakers. But once again Kobe is different. He has started his own line of clothing, written 16 rap songs for an album, and has more than one million registered fans in his fan club, which donates nearly all its membership dues to charity.

In spring 2000, Kobe once again proved how different he was by spending more than a million dollars to purchase the best professional basketball team in Italy, Olimpia Milano. He named his father the head of basketball operations and plans to be an active owner in between NBA seasons.

Kobe has started his own line of clothing, written 16 rap songs, and has more than one million registered fans in his fan club.

It is clear that Kobe has a vision of where his life is leading and what he wants to do. He has said that he wants to one day get married, win an NBA championship, and then raise his family in Italy, where he can have a closer relationship with the team he now owns.

"I've got a vision, but exactly what it encompasses and where it will lead, I'm not sure," Kobe said. "I just want everybody to sit back and enjoy the ride."

It has been a wonderful though short ride so far. Kobe's sure to treat basketball fans to many more years of high-flying dunks, impressive ball handling, and maybe even a championship or two.

It is clear that Kobe has a vision of where his life is leading and what he wants to do.

Chronology

- Born August 23, 1978 in Philadelphia, Pennsylvania
- Family moves to Italy in 1984
- In 1991, family returns to the United States
- In 1996, named High School Player of the Year; enters NBA draft; in July, the Los Angeles Lakers trade Vlade Divac for Kobe
- 1997, named to the NBA All-Rookie Second Team; wins slam dunk contest
- 1998, Becomes youngest player ever to start in an NBA All-Star Game; becomes starting guard for Lakers
- Buys professional basketball team in Italy in 2000

Index

South Campus
White Bear Lake Area High School
3551 McKnight Road
White Bear Lake, MN 55110